A hen is sitting on
the hay in the shed.

The hen gets up.
The hen has an
egg on the hay.

The next day the hen
has two eggs on the
hay.

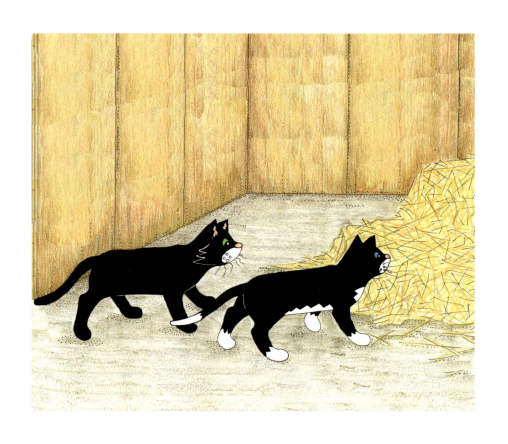

Jelly and Bean go
to play in the shed.

'You cannot play,'
said the hen. 'I am
sitting on my eggs.'

Kevin and Lotty go
to see the hen sitting
on the eggs.

The cats and dogs
go to see the hen
every day.

Then the eggs crack
and the hen has two
little chicks.